Outbursts From The Seventh Decade

A Collection of Poems by

Carol Chapman

OUTBURSTS FROM THE SEVENTH DECADE:

A COLLECTION OF POEMS BY CAROL CHAPMAN

Printed in the United States of America

ISBN: 979-8-218-37385-6

Editor: David Nazario

Cover design: Idalmi Rivera

Manhattan

Sitting in a bus, I imbibe
a cocktail of yellow, black, brown, and white
marvel at the blend of variation and similarity
expressionless or vivacious, loud or silent
a human cocktail.

Acknowledgements

Thank you to David Nazario for making this happen, and love to friends near and far for your encouragement and support.

Table of Contents

The muse visits and the mind reflects.

Gift of Touch

Human beings have five peerless GPS
environmental interpreters: sight, smell, hearing,
taste
and unheralded touch

Pleasure, pain, texture, temperature
compliments of touch intertwined with skin
delivers a caress or a slap

Touch, our palpable connection to people
a conduit to our emotional core

Hands greet…cheeks touch… lips kiss
bodies rub
casual or intense
contact is a charged means of communication

Touch is a messenger delivering compassion
acknowledging the corporal dimension of life
Touch, short circuited diminishes life
like gloves that separate the fingers

from the tangibility of a surface or human flesh

No surprise that Michelangelo depicted the Creation of Adam

an extended finger

and a reaching hand…the touch of life.

Faces

We stare at faces on monuments
trying to find traces of the person
immortalized
A bronze surface deflects and exalts
So we look, but we do not see
When we are looking at each other
an opportunity to see is at arm's length
Physical attributes are the easiest to discern
A mole next to an eye
commanding nose
lusty or pert lips
salon contoured or unruly eyebrows
lips that pucker, sneer, or snarl
Eyes — the Geiger counter that pings, guides
us beyond the surface
Direct, evasive, riveting, or empty
eyes are incapable of dissembling

Follow the web of a life lived or denied
Expressionless faces encased in permafrost or
rutted
Faces refracting moonbeams bouncing off
violins — yearning or capitulation
As we sit around the table there is no bronze

or stone here

Someone is reading our tantalizing margins
seeking our vulnerability while waltzing with
our eyes

Slide Show

Lately
My mind functions like a slide projector
Equipped with a carousel
Loaded with images like hieroglyphics
inscribed in stone
Sundry moments distilled by time
Buried in the arc of a life

Now I am bobbing in a sea of driftwood
Floating helter-skelter
Endlessly trolling in crevices, roiling memory

Behind my eyes a tantalizing slideshow
resurrects scenes lived:
Whizzing down a hill seated on a bicycle bar
Whooping fearlessly, with a brother
who navigates flawlessly
Mystery of an ice cream cake surrounded by
steamy cubes, hot to the touch
Listening to LP's on a library phonograph,
earphones in place
Lawrence Ferlinghetti's blaspheming upsets
household, empowering me with the response:
"It's poetry!"

I am stunned by the mind's crystal clear
projections
Pulling me into a chamber no longer sealed
A slide show has commenced aided by
silent, solitary moments
Under the spell of Corona.

Time Warp

Time stands still while moving
forward, contradicting itself by
forming a circle: Days, weeks, months
Unrelentingly turn calendar pages
while anchoring us to a circle of routinized
momentum — reality in disconnect
Sometimes the circle makes an unexpected
detour, daring to become a right angle
An angle of commonality
Where masked strangers lift their eyes
seeking the time they traveled unencumbered
as fearless, unsuspecting voyagers on life's
roller coaster
Eye contact outwits six degrees of separation
closing the gap Corona's virulent rays inflict
A precious human connection
a magical moment
acknowledging that life rushes by in a vacuum
Two strangers form a right angle
knowing that times circle thwarts the orbit of
their lives

...Pause

...then press rewind — walk naked or clothed
with or without shoes
in water
sand, dry or moist soil
... inhale earth's sweet breath — like the top of
a newborn's head
feel embraced by a bountiful earth
teeming with microorganisms and homo
sapiens
avoid nature's enticing snares — draw
sustenance from nature's lush foliage
cocooning the earth —
fear and admire four- legged creatures
in earth's unspoiled pockets
marking territory — when fluttering wings of
birds and insects are stilled by wind and rain
whipping through treetops — listen to nature's
dissonance
Pause...
heed the messenger's doleful song

If Only...

A plumb line measures verticality
while a level measures horizontally
tools relied upon for exactness
Flush with a wall
a level or plumb line never lies
As the expression goes – nothing can be true
unless it is on the level
If only people could be measured like a wall
deception and soft shoeing would be
discovered
like a bowed wall lacking integrity

To the naked eye the wall may be smooth,
uncompromised
but a craftsman's tool reveals defects and
inconsistencies
If only penetrating eyes looking into a mirror
like the plumb line or level
could measure deceit, melting a dissembler's
façade
Defects heightening the compromised wall
no longer masked, would bubble to the surface
Glibness would mock itself
and like the bowed wall

crumble, leaving debris and regret

Frederick Douglass Howls

Noose of racism tightens
bullets and chokeholds
No peace when one man kneels on the neck of
another
Lady justice holds lopsided scales
Blindfold slumping around her neck
while Black men and women are deprived of
life
to become a #
scrolled with a litany of names

Crawling across eyeballs

of anesthetized viewers

Time to shout-out the names of the victims
Men and women manhandled
Crushed by disregard
indifference
and seething hatred
A reflection of self-hatred

Peer into the mirror of judgment
Take a long penetrating look beyond the

superficiality of White or Black
Introspection cannot remove scars or rewrite
history
It can eviscerate falsehoods by peeling away
the epidermis
Transcending race, leaving humankind to
forge anew
Nat Turner can no longer be put on hold
His specter will rise from ashes
searing the oppressors' eyeballs
dissolving chains of color and caste

Fire Not Ice

CONSIDER…

17 parched African
nations Telescope bloated
children with fire in the
belly

CONSIDER…

polar bears adrift
not on floating
ice
Bemoan frantic seals without a place to rear
pups
Pity the survivors of Paradise's inferno
Lives scorched and upended
Ask Fox News about the fire-breathing
dragons ablaze in orange and yellow
on the plains of MAGA

CONSIDER…

123 degrees on sub-continent India
Smell shriveling human flesh
as dragons encircle the planet mocking
and scorning Gaea
Titans of the Anthropocene Age

decreeing fire not ice.

CONSIDER...

Trilobite

Some say that self-determination is an
illusion — A statement I debunked having
observed how adolescents plunge into the
arena of life
Many from stifling circumstances
Taking control
Wrestling with burlap sacks that tormented
parents
Unbelieving teachers and society's
indifference impose
Intensifying the Promethean struggle without
squelching unflinching will

Unflinching will
Pride in self-determination
Who or what can paralyze the unfettered
spirit?
Olympian god or insidious microbe reveling in
front of cowering beings

Frighted like the pilot spiraling from a giddy
height
with as much control as the trilobite on its way
to extinction
Feeling the constraints of an endless pause
Impulse and instinct aborted, riveted

Mocked by the notion of endless options
deprived of untethered mobility: I confess I
am in LOCK DOWN

Free Fall

Being hostage to Covid 19 demands surrender
of mobility, freedom of choice
and curtailment of desire
Even though
Books, mags, streaming, and texting place the
mind in a captive's holding zone
It clings to its cluttered world and manages to
survive

But it is the hushed moments that trigger a
fugue
A mind in free fall seeking awareness
Trying to understand how one situation relates
to another
Society's flaws scrutinized, magnified
Scored under the microscope of Corona
I am isolated, but not incarcerated and
in isolation
Calendar days seem unending, but not
meaningless
I am not a prisoner in a suffocating cell

Human contact, zilch
Mental stimulation, zilch

In the 21st century an isolation stranglehold
a barbaric solution, like waterboarding
solving nothing
a mindless punishment in the name of law and
order
Being isolated by Covid 19 is a mild sentence
Being a prisoner in isolation is a living death

Friendship

Friendship like bone tissue
can have a hard outer shell
deflecting tensions
disagreements
temperamental differences
while protecting ego and a lifetime's clutter.

But beneath the shell
lies a network of channels
nourishing a nexus of breath-taking
experiences
intertwined thinking and jarring
contradictions.

This taut embrace supports, shapes, and
nourishes vulnerable flesh
during a perilous hopscotching journey
through life.

Navigating this journey requires healthy
spongy marrow
to absorb the nutrients of friendship's
challenges and rewards.

Friendship is a transplant from narrow confines
to a burgeoning terrain where discoveries are endless.

Ring-Around-The Rosie

Lives unravel as wily Covid spins a black veil
Enabled by cavalier mortals

Covid circumvents prophylactic measures
Wields his scythe before him

Like an image in a memento mori painting
An unrelenting mantra: testing, gowns, masks,
ventilators

Covid gloats as saner entreaties sputter
Grinning while politicians pander

Covid clips the wings of the angels among us
Kingpins genuflect before financial markets
exchanging life for lucre and scepter

Leaving the playing field to Covid
Machiavelli winks: brilliant strategy
Covid will thin the herd of politically incorrect
voters.

Ring-around-the Rosie, a pocket full of posey
Ashes, ashes we all fall down: DEAD.
Let's have another rally….

Loss Multiplied

In a lifespan losses sting in degree
Like a burn
Loss of dignity — a first-degree burn
Fosters introspection leavened with humor

Loss of purpose — a second-degree burn
Challenges us to reinvent ourselves
Losses multiply — propelling us forward
Like a flip book until the ultimate loss leaves
us leaden
Benumbed, a player in blind man's bluff

Tagged by Corona personally or by extension
a third-degree burn sears our landscape
Now littered with markers as losses multiply

America Out of Tune

White, privileged, wealthy
powerful victimizers protecting turf
Chuckling as middle and lower orders
scramble for scraps
Cackling as blame flashes
Black deflecting inadequacy
vigilantes tighten the circle
exclaiming white supremacy

History glorifies tales of dominance
with valor, creating a mythology
of white exceptionalism and entitlement
Columbus slaughters the Taino
Custer slaughters native Americans
engorging the myth of preeminence

Whiteness is the gold standard
Disenfranchising Black, Brown, and Yellow
Leaving human rights out of the equation
Overlooking how Black blood spawned white
wealth
How Black sinews toiled while vigilantes
enshrined White rights

Deluded by racial purity hokum
the land professing freedom became
the land of the white
whiteness as a passport

In the decade of Covid-19
vigilante mentality remains unaltered
People of color, expected to cross the moat
perform essential services, ignore the lack of
medical and economic parity
while thrusting themselves into the eye of the
pandemic

Placing a knee
on the windpipe of George Floyd
the same knee
that enslaved people felt in Jamestown
Vigilantes of 2020
riddled with racist toxicity
reinforced by lame justice stoke the weeping
wound
Another limp Black body adds to the litany of
wrongful deaths
causing volcanic eruption, spotlighting the
cavernous moat
perpetuated by the illusion of superiority

Racism cries out for a vaccine inoculating

against hatred and violence afflicting mankind
Vigilantes must become the Eumenides bestowing
justice
or there will be no harmony, no fraternity

only rubble raining down

Wine and Roses

The word love is overdosed and wrapped in
vanity.
It is pushed, crushed, and left to dry out like
play-doh.
The four-letter word rolls off the tongue and
hits the floor with a thud,
yet floats in the air like milkweed.

Could it be that the Greeks understood the
breadth of the frayed word,
and rejected sloppy sentimentality in a capsule
labeled love?

Agape, philia, eros: the Greeks parse love's
dimensions
attempting to chart its shiftiness focusing on
family, friendship, passion.

A bleached word, leaches out love's key
ingredients, trust and fidelity, leaving drooping
roses, musty wine,
and love-less self.

Diving

Love comes in different guises
Sometimes it paints with a fiery red palette
Waxing scarlet to purple
An intractable purple takeover
Like snorkeling without water
Subsuming the primary color
Sealing it in an oxygen-less tank
Fermenting chemical changes —
Rupturing a lifeline.

What Is It Like to Be Chained by Circumstance?

Light still streams into a room,
Cleansing, dressing, adorning, as usual
Earrings never neglected

No external sounds resonating,
Only the prism of Arvo Part's minimalist music
Bathing the senses.

Friends detached....voices become sterile
Embalmed words encased in a device

Inducement to dash into the street cauldron nullified
Invigorating gallery hop in Chelsea now a chimera

Tormenting thoughts of a lover
Floating in a fishbowl of exile
Cannot be expunged

Just drifting in a timeless vacuum
confronted by circumstance's deadbolt
Waiting and longing for release from life in
stasis

Redemption

Limned in grisaille or basking in virgin clouds
our city's bugle call stirs its inhabitants

A collective heartbeat is a story in
motion until a thunderbolt is hurled in its
midst
Its presence a landmine
and the bugle call fades like extinguishing
lights
Taps at a grave site, as the mourners shuffle
off to grieve, trying to comprehend the
meaning of this sudden arbitrary shift.

Now a story in slow motion emerges,
as the tempo of life gutters

and heartbeats sputter, an indomitable
will emerges, lifted by those who are
marshaled, each and everyone firmly in
place.

Doctors, nurses, medical technicians
fulfilling their mission.
Young people stocking shelves,
truck drivers delivering food,
maintenance crews, civil servants,

people of different stamps and stripes
refusing to let the story end.
A color-blind heartbeat becomes a collective
will, and may...be a story of redemption.

Zip Up

Our nation, a split zipper
no longer drawn together by the wedge

Government divided — violated
rending from within and without

Tracts no longer insuring connectivity
Self-serving rhetoric mocking a revered
chamber
encouraging tyranny.

Shuttered eyes, turned heads
massaging violence
unleashing tsunami waves

Even after desecration, legislators peddle
falsehoods
spurning truth and reason

Blatantly gloss over the onslaught against
democracy,
forgetting the camera's eye is one with the
viewers.

Exorcize the seditionists within and without
Our wedge: The Constitution bequeaths us the
rule of law.

Bring back statesmanship, resist tyranny, align
the tracks —

ZIP UP NOW

Wilderness

The master bites the plate twice
First incising the images of individualized
faces into copper

Shrieking eyes, contorted mouths
a looking glass of sorrow, cruelty, resignation,
pain

Men, women swallowed by war, recklessness,
folly
A mordant bite into the viewer's retina

"You Can't Look," but we do look at victims,
torturers, hypocrites, sadists

Goya draws the viewer into the wilderness
Human catastrophes carried on the back of an
ass
from one century to another

Reason in a coma while monsters are boldly
etched into our consciousness

Goya dips his plate into acid exposing the
guilty twins:
Silence and indifference

Song For a Just Nation Begins

In the playground — children laughing,
shoving, hugging,
becoming adults embracing love of other
Shunning and obliterating deadend voices

No longer stymie our laborers — soldiers of
our workforce
with puny wages and dismissiveness

Respect must translate into equal remuneration
and opportunity
for women, and men minus a skin tone litmus
test

Discredit low-minded assertions factoring
working-class people
as COGS: Cost of Goods Sold
Instead factor them as partners in the future of
a thriving economy

In sickness and health, a nation as mother and
father
providing medical care from birth to death

abandoning none
A healthy nation sings from the diaphragm
sending its clarion
voice around the world

Educate in the key that suits students while
providing exposure
to all the songs and possibilities before them

Careful not to ignore art, literature, and music
from all cultures
offering their narrative through their voices

Voices expressing recognizable thoughts
and emotions
revealing closeness and kinship

America sings its song for a just nation in a
new tempo
a celebration offering a hallelujah

Fever Dream

Is it a fever dream?
Males asserting ownership
Spearheading an assault on women's bodies

Is it a fantasy of a wannabe enslaver?
White patriarchal society claims sovereignty
for pleasure, power, and profit
Enslaved Black women were chattel and
pawns
Pinioned these women could not rebel
when their bodies were violated

Men granted permission to spill
their seed willy-nilly
while in a stupor Big Brother monitors female
genitals
legislating away jurisdiction over reproductive
organs —
responsibility and decision making denied

Eviscerate and enslave women —
human rights for men, but not the skirt
Women's bodies are not feverish delusions
or pawns for male shifting

and political angling

Listen up: the vagina is a Queen — not a pawn
in a fever dream
No commanding away a woman's freedom to
exert ownership of her body with a whip or a
gavel

WOMEN ARE
DEMANDING EQUAL
RIGHTS

ASPHYXIATE THE FEVER
DREAM — NOW

Crosshairs

Death is like a loaded die for Black people
Assassin-bullets target faces —
Black and Yellow in the crosshairs.
Outcome assured like dots on the weighted
cube.
One out of six faces might be collateral
damage.
A random victim's whiteness dissolves as
bullets
ricochet like hailstones.
Ragged-edged hatred leaves an abattoir in its
wake.
Media frenzy packages atrocity, political
platitudes regurgitated
Deflects blame — ignoring a groundswell of
racism.
In the land of the free tossing a die into
churches,
Spas, nail salons — just a bad day.
John Wilkes Booth was having a bad day on
April 14,1865.
Who cares about FOUR SCORE AND
SEVEN YEARS AGO…
Eventually no one will escape the weighted
die.

Whoredom

In an age of gender fluidity
whore is a word rife for correction

Time to sluff off the Magdalene curse — hurl
the whore label at Adam

Frighted by women of purpose and intellect
men liberally smear them
knowing the stain lingers
Wretched women selling their bodies for coin

What about men selling their souls for prized
football tickets
first-class flights
insider trading

Women with ambition and focus reviled by
male smugness
fueled by phallic presumption

She is the whore of Babylon;
He is King David
Did you say whore?

Race-baiting, caged children, Corona
falsehoods,
climate change denial wrapped in a male-
centric worldview
swimming in decadence

In the fraternity of whoredom
male whores prosper

Nothing new, just a word rife for correction.

Rivalry

It is whispered on Mount Olympus that Apollo
tortured Marsyas for hubris.

Umm, maybe the Olympian god, slayer of
Python, resented the upstart.

A mortal playing the aulos enchanting the
muses
while Apollo clutched his beloved lyre.

The celebrated God of music, irritated by the
competition
turned his lyre upside down producing dulcet
tones.

Marsyas' one mouthpiece wind instrument
cannot compete.
Wiley Apollo triumphs and exacts his revenge.

Marsyas bound, flayed alive by the god of sun
and light.

Sparklers Not Rockets

What happened to rockets bursting in air?
A team of astronauts dazzled as one left
his footprint on the moon's surface

Silicon Valley thrust the world into a new
sphere with lightning connectivity

Eyes of the world respectfully focused on
transition of leadership
stunned by images of mayhem like a third-rate
American movie

Nationhood demeaned and traumatized as
sedition
snakelike
Struck with deadly venom the aorta of
democracy

Conspiracy theories disseminated through the
veins of the citizenry
Guileless minds tainted, whipped into a frenzy
discharging a torrent of bile

A seat of power aided by a rogue's gallery
shredding our constitution, abetting a seditious
coup
inflicting a gut-wrenching blow to the nation's
foundation

A senator sworn to uphold the constitution,
fist in the air
fuels marauders steeped in the cult of
MAGA...morphing
in real time into Marauders Attacking Glorious
America
Sparklers may commemorate the failed plot
against democracy
But will the rockets ever be hailed again?

Art of Letting Go

When we fly
We abandon the ground beneath our feet
We ignore the feeling of flying
Tugging at our discomfort

Life is a wanderer's flight
Requiring sidestepping
Resisting familiarity

Should we be eyeing the heights
Or avoiding edges and corners
Sealing out the emotional cliff
Circle or Ziggurat

Choices mold our disposition
Stay within the calcifying circle
Or grasp the edges of the
Ziggurat
And feel exhilaration while letting go!

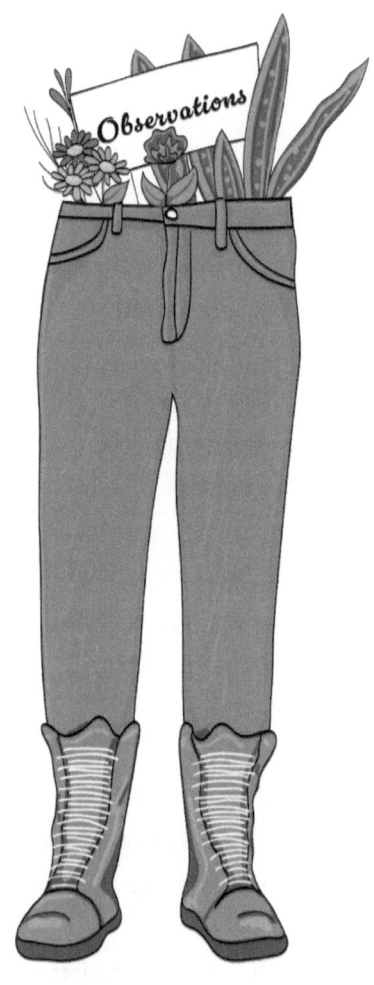

Observing is like listening....it requires attentive eyes and ears.

Night Rambling

Darkness descends drawing the curtain
forming a rim like a Mason Jar blocking light.
Buildings are silhouettes with empty blistered
slits
frequently spotlighting framed figures in
pantomime
Street crossings glare like whiteout
yellow-red sculptural objects hang in space
Cardboard lean-to shelters occupant from
frosty
chill and prying eyes
Windup creature darts from billowing
mountains
avoiding ominous biped.
Deli flower stalls defy abandoned storefronts
splashing dabs of color
Strangers become shadows in the beam of
night sentinels
Faces become shadow box cameos on black
velvet
Rambling in the night city is an inkblot test
shifting shapes
teasing the flaneur whose eyes are the
spotlight

Masquerade

Seared by a streetscape eerily devoid of
clamor, city dwellers, mindful of a dance
macabre unfolding
in their midst, decided to join the masked ball.
Vibrantly colored, logo strewn, wildly
designed or repurposed, a mask allowed
people to reclaim the hushed streets and
avenues of their city.

They believed that the force had awakened,
bequeathing them the masked ball as their wall
of protection.
But the wall had insidious cracks that began
to spread.
Mask-less marauders were rejecting the
force's shield,
wearing defiant smirks or an air of
nonchalance.

Deftly trying to escape the wake of the
mask-less,
zigzagging and meandering to avoid the
perimeter of contagion, fearful of rebuking
the scoffers

the masked knew they were neutralized.
Protective wall breached by arrogance
paraded before their eyes.

The masked understood: the force's strength
depended on an impenetrable wall.
To defeat the danse macabre…
the mask-less must
empower the force by saying, I bite my thumb
at death, close ranks and join the masquerade.

Warrior

Her rage like poison ivy leaches out
Screaming, "You fuckers!"

Pushing her wheelie — assault and barrier
Her path mowed — mower blades unhinged
censuring inhabitants in an unrelatable world

Isolation, fear oozing from her pores
Lips cataloging complaints
Eyes growling
Daring engagement

A hunched warrior battle-scarred —
Lear in the wilderness, fraying like thread-bare
fabric
Passersby shield themselves —
Withdraw like threatened octopuses
Cocooning themselves, maintaining distance

Deprived of recognition
the babbler's voice weakens — fades away
Another warrior instantly dismissed and
forgotten

Signals

Receiving a gift plant leaves me feeling
ambivalent
A thriving yellow flower cosseted in leafy
green
Demands attention and nurturing
Seeing that lone flower in front of my sunny
window
Compels me to acknowledge its presence
I sit facing the window, occasionally glancing
In its direction, reading its body language
Picturesque petals signal vitality
A wistful posture signals neglect, urgency
A stooping head, the final plea
Requires an act of resuscitation
Water must flow cautiously to avoid
drowning a once pert flower
To my astonishment my flower refuses to
succumb
Its head slowly cranes upward
Startled by nature's resilience, my thoughts
stretch
Ensuring survival of a gift requires an engaged
response
Neglected flowers among us sound a similar
alarm.

Simon Says:
Playtime

Gather round…stakes are high

place hands on heads   seal lips
even if you lose   you win
      most coveted circles: greed

                 fraud

                 treachery

genuine or slithery commands
    only a moron would ask a stupid question
Simon says believe this… or...believe that…
A FACT IS NOT A FACT
INACTION IS... REALLY ACTION
      DEMOCRACY SUBSUMED BY
      OLIGARCHY
RACISTS ARE GOOD PEOPLE
      SENIORS WILL SWAP LIFE FOR

LOOT

JOURNALISTS ARE

SCUM

POLITICAL AGENDA... PARDON
LOYALISTS
CRONYISM: GET OVER IT

COVID 19 IS LOSING

DEATH TOLL VERSUS STOCK
MARKET

MEDAL OF FREEDOM
SLUT SUPPORTS HEALTH CARE

WHO'S LEFT STANDING?
S I M P L E   S I M O N

Besmirched Lady

Spurn the homeless
Turn away imploring arms, contorted faces

Stomp on prostate bodies
Wrench babes from sheltering mothers

Traumatize the innocent,
leaving them in limbo
Muffle sounds of sobbing children

Pack your eye sockets
with hate
Turn up the volume

Fill your ears with electrifying slogans
Immigrants — past, present, and future

Unfurl from your shroud
Diminished lamp, drooping lady

Scream and wail Lady
Scream!

Before My Eyes

Outside my window a forlorn yellow slide
trumpets its presence.

A ladder rope dangles minus elfin feet.
Listless swings decorate the play area.

Appealing weathered benches languish
in corners without company.

No boisterous voices reach my ears
like cymbals clashing in the air.

Before my eyes, majestic green shrubs
in cylindrical planters, salute like an honor
guard without a piper to lead the parade.

Playtime tucked away awaiting a carefree
day. I am the survivor of absence hungering
for unbridled children dodging and eluding
Corona's lethal crown.

I am one with them feeling the razor edge
whittling away discoveries magically
unfolding.

Together we climb the ladder rope so that we
cannot be sucked into the maelstrom.

Viola's

Ring the buzzer for entry to Viola's Smart Shop
enticingly modern and old-fashioned

A dominative lioness, soft-spoken voice,
snap in her step
grants access.
New dress too diaphanous for volunteer gig,
mini-white slip, out of a well-worn cardboard box brings
a sigh of relief.
Proprietor, well into her ninth decade, always intent,
radiates like a fan unfurling.

Visited Viola's for her singular personality,
pert manner, as well
as her fashionista sensibility.
A curator of the finest lingerie, eager to surf in boxes or antique
drawers containing womanly delights.

Standing before a gated storefront with a plastic sleeve

containing paper and pencil for comments,
empty windows…minus Viola's pizzazz,
admonishing me for not popping in before a
three-day absence.

 An independent spirit's dominion whisked
away
Another casualty under the umbrella of
Corona.

Snow Romance

Dizzying pearl drops or fluttering moths
falling out of a gray-wash sky
Roof tops trimmed with crown molding.
Fire escapes dressed in fluffy cool whip,
Snow's urban installation teasing the eye.

Romance begins to deconstruct like a Banksy
Once the populace emerges.
Booted feet draw trenches through snow-white
canvas.
Snow blowers, shovels, snow plows reinforce
deconstruction
following the cleanup brigade.

Curbside igloos become fortresses awaiting
rescue.
Snow tossed in the street, recycled - landing
where it began.
Children roll around leaving body imprints
while pets leave sun-flower signatures.
Salt pellets like scavengers eat everything in
their path.
Street corners become the pedestrian triathlon.

Festooned trees understand the burden of
romance
their limbs weighted with snow.
Snow that will surely melt away.

Pocket Park Retreat

Feeling the urge to escape my enclosure
I set out early on a brisk, sunny morning
and followed my usual loop from York
to Park.

On a whim I stopped for coffee
intending to return home and sip reverently.

But the invigorating air made me eager
to prolong my feeling of liberation.

So, I decided to check out the pocket park.
Set back from the street
ample and fronted by steps
it is frequently overlooked.

Sure enough...not a soul in sight.
Chose a spot between two impressive
planters potted with Galway-green shrubs.

Removed my mask, and felt the breeze
on my face

a mask-less novelty

Silence and emptiness made me
feel like a figure in a de Chirico
painting
not even a sparrow in sight.

The giant, rough-hewn planters became
props in an Italian piazza.
But one of the planters was empty,
it took on a dimension of simplistic beauty
arte povera unembellished
just a physical presence in a space.

My morning in a pocket park became an
exhilarating museum experience on 79th
Street.

Cluster

Sidewalks dotted with makeshift bars
Walk by...size up the scene
chat
smile
laugh

shoulder to shoulder
drinking beer
wine
cocktails
frozen
margaritas

Tongue wets thirsty lips
not only for my seasonal margarita
but for restless abandon insulated by
dismissiveness
fueled by youthful energy

Cluster of madness
— yes—
defying an opaque windshield
harmless in a rearview mirror

Unsettled by push-pull tugging at caution
sparks of envy torment the ageless spirit
lamenting loss and folly

Fugitives

Wind a keyed mantel clock
And a reassuring tick…tock
With an alluring and intruding hourly chime
Eventually recedes like white noise absorbed
In the flow of time

Replace the pendulum with coiled metal
moving hands joined at noon and midnight

Minute hand pirouettes with a persistent
Pulse sweeping sixty seconds to countdown

Severed hands acquiesce to digits
Boldly amping up hours and minutes declaring
deadlines

No more soothing sand rendering another sixty
minutes gone
The hourglass and humankind intertwined
Frozen in the moment…fugitives of time.

Kettle to Kettling

My tea kettle sits on my stovetop with its lid
Decorative handle beckoning
Simply a benign cauldron
Steam escapes through the spout
Boiling water seeps my tea bag

Kettling with its kinship to kettle
Evokes a different reality
Peaceful protesters corralled
Encircled by police officers closing ranks
Squeezing faceless people into a cluster

A military-style phalanx with shields
Chemical sprays, batons aloft, kettling
Bystanders and protesters

Blurred outlines
No longer citizens
exercising their first amendment right
To assemble peacefully

Instead, kettled citizens seeking daylight in
madness
No safety valve, no escape hatch, no rational
objective
Corralled and kettled before the eyes of the
world

Wonderland

Walking in the park my body leaning forward
with each step
Signaling absorption and intent
Even though directionless

My eyes seeing trees decked out
in dizzying splendor
Mirthfully mocking me
with commanding girth
Rooted in an embracing stance

I am like Giacometti's skeletal figures
Walking in emptiness

A specter of my former self
A diminished face avoiding other cloaked
faces seeking protection
Grouped and alienated
A frightened species walks vigorously to assert
identity
Desperately looking for empathy and
recognition
From other manikins walking to affirm their
strength in the faceless wonderland

We walk to escape and look to the permanence
of comforting trees

Mirage On Allen Street

A bus ride on Allen - a long, funky street, is a
documentary
in slow motion

There are gleaming storefront interlopers that
catch the eye
But nothing like the stagecraft on the side of
an old comfort station

Two elegant chairs
A centered coffee table
An end table with a perched wine glass

The delicate placement of a straw hat trimmed
with a black band
adorns one of the chairs
It mirrors the way my hat is lovingly placed

Upstage is a wooden platform supporting a
sleeping bag
with a woman lying flat on her back
A large black umbrella is her protective
awning

On the wall behind her, a street mural
decorates her
comfort station
RRDF, the tag of the artist, in bold letters
offsets fading
mirthful images of three women in a circle

My camera captures this arresting scene
without this image
it would have been a mirage on Allen Street

Moving Van

A moving van pulls up and parks in front of a
house
No for sale signs or harried agents case the
property
No anxious buyers circling, only the gigantic
van
The van becomes a looming presence; its
mission inevitable but undeclared
Movement begins in slow motion: chairs
circling each other in a final performance
without an encore
recede into a cavernous
cargo bay through the side door.
Walls tremble discovering their nakedness:
photographs,
paintings, prints feel the absence of
worshiping eyes –
one by one they hesitantly join the chairs.
Objects large and small without a caress
dissolve into effervescence.

Frayed spines etched with incomprehensible
squiggles, unlovingly stacked to be pawed by
unfamiliar hands, succumb. Colors blend
becoming an indistinguishable

wash while all lighted lamps
refuse to dim becoming lanterns resisting the
engorging van poised
to move on to another location.
Muted the house's timbers settle, a hushed
figure's feet barely
touch the floor when the van's door slams
shut

Screed

In the time of fiction
Film imagery becomes reality on real-time TV

A harrowing harangue devolves into a
meltdown
A man in the throes of histrionics

Black dye streaking down a cosmeticized face
Driven by obsession, ignoring an engulfing
contagion

Clinging to an orgiastic fantasy sugar-coated
with power lust
A face and mouth caricaturing itself blithers
bunkum
Frantically mopping sulfurous sweat
Unleashing a stream of black from his skull

A corrupted press conference peddling
falsehood, speaking in tongues
Referencing the film, *My Cousin Vinny*
While giving life to a scene from *Death
in Venice*
A twisted mind, devoid of rationality

Delivers a petrifying performance which
freezes the blood

Agonistes spinning demagoguery
The audience gasps
Confronted by the darkness lurking in a man's
soul

AN INDELIBLE FINAL CUT

Recognition

My aging hands have sinews like tree limbs
Spidery tendons
meander in different directions

Intricate avenues stand out — hands and tree
branches have distinct but similar signatures

Lifting my hands, I compare the byways on
my hand
with the outline of tree branches silhouetted
on pavement

Some lift upwards
Others bend and curve
Like the furrows on my hands — both refuse
to bow

Sitting on a bench under the canopy of trees
Nature's shadow and my shadow reveal our
commonality

Amaryllis

Peeking over the edge of my book
my eyes focus on my amaryllis

Millimeter by millimeter
inching from its protective sheath
it refuses to thrust itself forward – no hasty
leap
circumspect
biding its time

Following nature's timing,
two peach flowers emerge
outliers eclipsing flamboyant red
poised on an erect stem, crowned with radiant
beauty

Blushing flowers soothing the harshness of
turmoil
in a hemorrhaging nation with no steady hand
on the rudder

Their stolid presence reigns in destructive
impulses
muting rebellion in a restive soul lashed to the

mast

Like the amaryllis embrace the dormant stage
Monitor turbulent waters
deride lunacy
gather strength
with determination and constancy

Eros's Mischief

Apollo smitten by Eros's golden arrow
fervently pursues Daphne, the river nymph
Chaste Daphne recoils and flees
The taut body of the nymph
desperately tries to evade the sun god's
passion

No longer shining stone
Bernini's chisel transformed marble into soft,
supple skin
A mesmerizing drama in breathing sculpture

Motion in stone
arms and legs
emoting perfection of form

Open-mouthed
the nymph pleads for release
Apollo's hand remains on Daphne's pale waist

The striking beauty of the two figures
belies the clash of wills

Bernini created a disquieting tableau

love lust rape
intertwined

Missteps

A toddler wobbles landing with laughter
Legs strengthen
Lessons accrue

Some stick like discarded gum
Others flap heedlessly

One step blithely overtakes another
Years lope then g a l l o p…

As the staircase lengthens
Risers taunt like mountain peaks

Missteps like pieces of stone
Form a mosaic — a testament
Illuminating a life

Blossoming

Nature dazzles us with her spring conjuring
trick
Pink and white blossoms in picture-perfect
bravura
command attention, leaving spindly trees for
another season

Yellow dandelions — daisy's cousins
poke diminutive heads
above mangy grass

Eventually tufts will be plucked, seeds blown
scattering wishes in the air

Forsythia's robustness pleases our eyes
tulips' color chart foreshadows pastel
costuming
Cyclical revival reaffirms nature's continuity

Leavening our step, charging our senses
Like sunflowers we lift our heads
turn our faces, hitch a ride
in Helios' chariot careening across the sky

Rock

Some call you boulder
But I call you rock

When you are alone
Your sprawling shape and honed texture rivets
the eye

A sculpture minus the chisel
Tired legs are thankful for your perch
Small feet scramble
Like adventurous mountain climbers to
Everest

You are a squirrel's gymnasium
Or a bird's landing pad
A rock of ages —
Stonehenge without mystical pretension
My unwavering Polaris
Fixed, silent, detached

Poppet Visits

She arrives like an unexpected spring breeze
Spreads her joy like refreshing dew drops
Steps into the spotlight
The show commences

Poppet scampers and swirls, defies gravity
Lifting and holding her legs in the air
A signature routine with endless twirling
Coyly performed to hook the audience

She is inspired when the tennis ball appears
A prop that alters her movements
Gleefully she pounces, playful attacks
No distress
When sparring partner retreats

Poppet is a prima donna minus a pedigree
Always ready for a cracker with a speck of
cheese
A tiny bundle of sunshine vanquishing
Corona's dreary palette

Coffee In the Rain

There is something satisfying about drinking
coffee in the rain
Nature's spritz is an air freshener
A rich aroma wafts through the moist air

Sitting on a café stool
heightens the senses
as droplets tickle my arms

Most people shun the opportunity to venture
out
Preferring coziness at home
avoiding puddles and wet surfaces

There are some like-minded individuals
who find the emptiness
in otherwise symphonic surroundings
a restful chamber setting

They might even acknowledge each other
exchanging a few words
without violating the sphere of contemplation

When nature's sprinkle becomes an insistent

patter
it is time to start walking home

Raise the umbrella
listen to rain's staccato rhythm
be thankful for waterproof sneakers

Sundial

Am I the gnomon casting a shadow on the
plate?
My shadow mocks me
as my physical presence occupies a lower
position in the sky

Time alters like a river whose current flows in
two directions
Midday casts short shadows with time before
it
Leaving the gnomon time to move with the
sun.

Every past is consigned to the diminishing
present
Ambling arm in arm with a lengthening
shadow
My gnomon is my timekeeper in the shade

Cloudscape

Looking at a sprawling canvas arching over
the earth
One must ask: Who is the daring artist
rejecting figurative fluffiness?
Bold striations regaling the eye
A masterful hand's brushstrokes

command bands of blue
Counterpointing stark whiteness

Some areas are highlighted by gray smudges
Leaching into white
Other areas are whimsically speckled and
stippled
To delight the eye

In another historical time this painting would
have been stamped degenerate
Created by a debauched artist deviating from
norms
Defying expectations
A cloudscape that exhilarates

cannot be allowed to muddy or eclipse
Cumulus clouds with definitive shapes

My City Exhales

Walking in the city I felt a blessing of evening
song.
Zephyrus toyed with my hat as I walked
West.
An exodus from the museum was teeming
with energy.
A tableau of masks inhaling a salutary breeze.
Companions lingered and took artful snaps
accompanied by giggles.
An impromptu performance before my eyes
canes, wheeled strollers, sprinters gyrating like
a compass needle locating direction.
The fountain's rim, seating for the onlookers…
a camera's stagecraft.

Put my camera back in my pocket. Inhaling
a collective CHI: an insuppressible life
force leads to the park.
Each bench has a narrative: family with a
father helping his son open his treat.
Mom fusses over baby in its portable nest.
Adjacent bench, man sleeping, ankles crossed,

shoes tucked under the bench.

Another shoeless man eyes his fellow bencher.

Fathers hoisting children above their heads.

My city exhales and the narrative is in a
camera's lens.

Comfort Zone

Internalizing stillness, inhaling invigorating
air by the flank of the gray-old lady
suspended above the little red lighthouse

Eagerly her legs keep pace with his
A slight hint of origin in his voice resonates
like the river's tongue caressing the shore

Anecdotes in a rush of words spark a chorus
of laughter
A frieze of sculptural forms spanning the
river's edge arrests our attention

Rocks and rubble
in anthropomorphic shapes emerge
seducing the eye
Forked limbs like a sky-reaching appendage
gesture imploringly declaring the ineffable

Inhaling hushed thoughts,
our pace slackens
Acknowledging that rambling has whet our
appetites

we scan the heights spotting a three-tiered
climb
to the harsher world

Offering the bend of his arm
together we surmount boundaries
Defying distance

Sessions

The Crane squatting on the corner of Sea
Street entices thirsty, weary, fun-loving
rovers

A wall plastered with pics of musicians and
vocalists
Counterpoints a long, stressed bar
Robust bartender eyes slight female figure
"Green Spot single pot Irish whiskey, for
sure."

Sidled into surround booth; man sitting nearby
Unravels swaddling, revealing two ivory-hued
pipes.
Props one on each leg with glee and intent.
Leans over and hands me one.
"Made from PVC pipe — feel the rough
holes…
cut them myself."

Places mouthpiece under his tongue
Palpable sound envelopes me
Other musicians saunter in — embracing
various instruments
No program
No advertising

No cell phones
Only… Timelessness and Apollo…
in the pub on
The corner of Sea Street

Dead-Letter Box

Messages floating through air
Connections severed
Slights meaningless
Bitterness neutralized
Reconciliation dangling

Apologies reverberate in the sender's ear
Emotions flutter crisscrossing
Aborting possibilities like dead leaves

Jaundiced relationships in air currents
Circle around the world
Petty human foibles metastasize

Strife over politics
       religion
       resources
Dialogue muted —
Lands in the dead-letter box
Solutions suspended hopelessly
Crisscrossing the globe
Causing the body politic to hemorrhage...

Final Act

Aging is an ongoing performance fulfilling a
shifting script
It is no longer perched backstage — it is
focused in the retina

Highlighting contrasting colors and images
Chairs are props waiting to be removed
While paintings, seemingly fixed, embrace
their domain —
Resisting the final curtain call

Various egos have traversed the undulating
boards
Some leave deeply-grooved footprints
Others leave no trace — not even a specter

A few sputter on their way to oblivion
While some ad lib to lengthen the final act.

Sauciness is life's salt while naughtiness is life's pepper.

Ode to a Refrigerator

Largely ignored, you were just a fridge tucked
in a corner
Maybe photos or post-it notes dressed up your
portal

Your presence began to assert itself when the
threat of a scourge became a reality

Now...you are iconic and indispensable
An urge to explore your recesses
Eying your contents
to be reassured that you are replete
draws the suppliant

You are now a destination that lures the
pilgrim providing comfort and relief
from the mesmerizing screens
dominating our lives

A path to your niche, no longer considered a
lowly corner

Incessantly tread, triggered by an elemental
human instinct: survival

You gleam as a hand reaches out to grasp your
handle
Gloating about your elevation in the life of a
mere mortal while a hand retrieves a tantalizing
bottle of Prosecco and lips cautiously rebuke
refrigerator idolatry with a timid
PHOOEY

Sassy ....

Bad Ass Woman
Confined she can never be

Classy…Sassy…Chic…
A playfully morphing chameleon

Can she be brainy and sexy too?
A siren awaiting a black minnow
Beachcomber between her legs

A sassy woman
Refuses to be defined

Bad Ass
magnetism
Bathed in mystery

Friend…Lover…Whore…
An intoxicating boundless galaxy

Tilt Right or Tilt Left

Adornment, ego trip, self-expression
all of the above and more
Hats draw strangers' eyes
Smiles and "smart hat" utterances

Each one casts an aura: outrageousness
                              assertiveness
                              elegance
                              whimsy

Occasions and caprice dictate choice:
                      1950's feathered embrace
                      retro boater nonchalance
                      fedora evocative scarlet
                      cloche   purple   cap
                      populism

No longer inanimate once possessed
A hat morphs with the wearer
Pulled menacingly toward the eyes
with film noir flair or slightly above
forehead openness

Tilted rakishly left or coquettishly right
Singular friends that create illusions, hilarity
and reinvention with Gatsby theatricality

I doff my hat to innumerable hats posing in
my closet
brimming with possibilities
Where is that Panama?

Phantom

When a limb is severed, the amputee feels its
presence even though it is no longer there

Sensations emanating from loss are palpable
like a phantom lover

A lover's tongue lapping from the fountain of
my clitoris
His lance heralding the golden river of
intimacy and youth

Is it possible to inhale another being without
exhaling?
Carnal and spiritual melding ... an intangible
covenant of affinity

Presence felt hauntingly without physical
manifestation
Ritual ablutions cannot rub out the imprint left
on the host

Untitled

Ours was an unbidden magnetic attraction
atoms in a chemical reaction releasing energy

We embraced the moment without reservation
One radiating electric red, the other cool lapis

A panther softly encircled my torso
Breaching a barrier, drawing me into a purple
zone

Ultimately, tormenting and fragmenting a
loving heart

Purple never dims.

Sex (In the Time of Corona)

My nose inhales your essence from your ears
to your groin
Ebony skin smooth like marble entices
fingertips like pilgrims seeking solace
My tongue strokes and crisscrosses your
body while my lips nip and nudge
hidden recesses
Lips clamoring for your eager mouth
moist and ravenous
My mouth imbibes and sucks your manhood
until we are meshed in a cocoon of rhapsody
while texting to comply with distancing in the
time of Corona

Red Chair

Placed before a window
allowing morning light to
stream
my chair grabs attention like Rothko red
Club shaped
it wraps some comfortably while others
are expelled like an ill-fitting shoe

I dance before it without an occupant until it
telegraphs the arrival of a forlorn panther

Blackness radiates like a beacon's light
the night black and red blend
while whiteness hauntingly
allures panther eyes
with a primal dance

Dancing
a ritual invitation
performed for one
whose measure merits esteem
embracing and being embraced
by the red chair

Absent or present the chair has his genetic
code

embedded in leather

With or without his

presence

a distinct aura emanates

from the red chair

Buoyancy

Survival in a world
Tilted off its axis —

             Cupid's betrayal

Resilience — a lifejacket
Tempering ardor
Removes the suffocating dome

Allowing the dropped
Egg to roll, to avoid
             Being smashed

Lift Up Your Feet

Listen to the beat
      Let it pulse in your brain
      Wash over your limbs —
An INVASION flowing through your veins
         internalize
         externalize
         music's persistent call

Lift up your feet
         DANCE

         FOR

the hungry, the sick, the persecuted, the
homeless
         FOR

         still bodies lacking empathy stifled by
         constipated minds
         in an evolving changing world

Be humble thankful embrace the music

LIFT UP YOUR FEET

> AND DANCE
> DANCE
> DANCE

With the dizzying thought of joining hands as others

> LEAP TO THEIR FEET

Pow Bam

National Geographic in technicolor
      An invasive image like a camera flash
Black men with quarter moons
Filtered through my retina
      Embedded in my hippocampus
Triggered and retrieved in an instant
      By the utterance: "no ass"
Glossy, hypnotic pages —
         intruded, startled, paralyzed

Until you faced me with your arresting lance
      Reenacting the evolution of
      humankind

Nestling together like magnetic spoons
      In the unsullied cradle before the
      spawning of

Racism and biological exclusion

Ode to an Oyster

Your shell is flat, round, oval, spiky —
an oyster's covering like a codpiece
protects and harbors delicacy

If you observe oyster eaters
their approach
to succulence differs

Puffy or flat an oyster sits in a liquid
brought to lips poised to imbibe
its intoxicating tang

An oyster... the ocean's lover... has subtle
sweetness
earthy undertones, creaminess or briny
assertiveness
Kumamoto's buttery texture
and alluring mantle seduces
For a small oyster, it courts with a deep shell

Slurping an oyster is like sex without
ardor It should be savored...unhurriedly
tongued nibbled and swallowed with gusto

Sam I Am

Politeness distilled
Mellifluous voice
Buttery tongue
Endless endearments: "love," "baby," "stay
safe"
Mapped the art of love, but not the art of
loving

Freeze dried emotionally, admittedly friendless
Perfectionist devoted to his craft, craving
accolades
Secretive, dodging and feinting in shadows

Fear of Covid-19 prompts talk of change and
mistakes
As infection recedes
Vows crumble
Renewal slinks backwards comfortably

Worshipful of Jamaica's Titan
Misplaces the wisdom of his cultural icon's
reverence
For love in all its guises and demands
Hear the voice of your bard

Coward: defined as a man who awakens love
without any intention of loving
Yeah, Man

Femme Fatale

Observe the male firefly
flickering, swooping, courting

A pulsating pattern of luminescent beauty
designed to lure his own species

But nature endowed the female firefly with
mimicry
Seeking preservation
She creates a false pattern
Amorous illusion attracts

The male is devoured.

Ode to a Penis

You are the jack-in-the pulpit whose shaft
stands at attention beckoning the eye
a moving dowsing rod

Never sheepish with its — I know you want it
stance
A shaft of connectivity seeking a
cup for its milky latte

With or without a cap
its sculptural design
has minimalist beauty

Some say it's feckless, questing for housing
Latin provides the clue: furnished with a tail
an ever present appendage
sensitive to sight, touch
quivering with vulnerability

Resting on its sac or rousing from slumber
its seductive form
a heady presence
like heated ambergris…
intoxicates

Pomegranate 613

Burnished red an imperfect
sphere poised on a round table
awaiting a knife's slice into its red
river

Violation or act of love?

Separating seeds from membrane
            One by One
An intruder exposing secret depths
Violating the succulent's endless bounty
While dissolving the self
In a contemplative motion of seduction.

Honeybee

A honeybee climbs into a flower
sucking nectar from the carpal

Moving from flower to flower
with a straw-like mouth
He drinks his life force
feeding to fill his sack

Some are drawn by shape, size or reward
offered by the nectar
sipped from a chosen flower's sanctity

Honeybee draws deeply —
quivering as he tastes his chosen flower

About the Author

Carol Chapman hails from New York City where she taught high school English and a Humanities course in an Outreach Program for Kingsborough Community College. She spent 20 years at MoMA in the Education Department, before moving to Visitor Services. While at MoMA Carol contributed to the Volunteer Newsletter and three of her poems were featured in the Summer 2020 issue.

Carol is a lover of poetry, art, music, and exploring New York City's neighborhoods, where she interacts with the people and the different rhythms surrounding her. She believes writing poetry is "an act of sharing the drama of the human condition in all its glory and folly."

When asked, Carol refers to herself as "a scribbler." In 2020, Carol's poem, "Kingston, Jamaica" - inspired by Fleet Street - was published in *The Jamaica Gleaner*.

www.ingramcontent.com/pod-product-compliance
Lightning Source LLC
Chambersburg PA
CBHW020405130626
46549CB00006B/2450